The Extinction Of Dinosaurs

By Shanay Gengan

Introduction

Dinosaurs, the majestic creatures that roamed the Earth millions of years ago, have captured the imagination of people for generations. From their diverse sizes and shapes to their mysterious extinction, dinosaurs remain a subject of fascination and curiosity. In this book, we embark on a journey to explore the many facets of these incredible reptiles, uncovering the truth about their lives, their sudden disappearance, and the lasting legacy they left behind.

We begin by delving into the different types of dinosaurs that once dominated the land, sky, and seas. From the massive, plant-eating *Brachiosaurus* to the swift, predatory *Velociraptor*, each species played a vital role in the prehistoric ecosystem. But what caused the sudden extinction of these mighty creatures? Was it the infamous asteroid impact, or were there other factors at play? We will explore the catastrophic event that forever changed the course of life on Earth—the asteroid strike that created the Chicxulub crater and its immediate, devastating effects.

Which dinosaurs were the first to perish, and who were the last survivors clinging to life in a drastically changing world? Through detailed research, we will uncover who may have endured the longest and what gave them an edge.

From the aggressive predators like *Tyrannosaurus rex* to the calm, gentle giants like *Stegosaurus*, we'll examine the most dangerous and the most peaceful of dinosaurs. We'll also introduce you to *Nigersaurus*, the dinosaur with an astounding 500 teeth, and the bizarre-looking *Therizinosaurus* with its enormous claws.

Our journey continues with a closer look at how dinosaurs reproduced, with detailed information on their eggs, nesting habits, and the care they may have provided for their young. We will also dispel many misconceptions that have clouded our understanding of these ancient creatures.

Finally, dinosaur bones hold vital clues to their biology and behavior. By studying fossils, paleontologists have uncovered the mysteries of how dinosaurs lived, grew, and interacted with their environment.

This book is a comprehensive guide for anyone eager to explore the world of dinosaurs—from their rise to their tragic fall, and everything in between.

In order to know more about the extinction of Dinosaurs, firstly we need to know who they were

Dinosaurs were a diverse group of reptiles that dominated the Earth for over **160 million years**, from the **Late Triassic Period** (about 230 million years ago) to the **end of the Cretaceous Period** (about 66 million years ago). They were part of a group called **Archosaurs**, which also included ancestors of modern crocodiles and birds. The name "dinosaur" comes from the Greek words **"deinos"** (terrible) and **"sauros"** (lizard), meaning "terrible lizard," though dinosaurs were not technically lizards.

Key Characteristics of Dinosaurs

Classification:

Dinosaurs are divided into two major groups based on their hip structure:

Saurischia ("lizard-hipped"): Includes two major subgroups—theropods (mostly carnivorous dinosaurs like *Tyrannosaurus rex*) and sauropodomorphs (long-necked herbivores like *Brachiosaurus*).

Ornithischia ("bird-hipped"): Includes herbivorous dinosaurs like *Triceratops*, *Stegosaurus*, and *Ankylosaurus*.

Evolution:

Dinosaurs evolved from earlier reptiles during the **Triassic Period**, about 230 million years ago. They became the dominant land animals during the **Jurassic Period** and continued to thrive until the **Cretaceous-Paleogene (K-Pg) extinction event**.

Modern birds are believed to be direct descendants of **small, feathered theropod dinosaurs**, making birds the only living dinosaurs today.

Physical Features:

Size: Dinosaurs ranged greatly in size, from small, bird-like creatures weighing less than a chicken (*Microraptor*), to giant herbivores like *Argentinosaurus*, which could reach lengths of over 100 feet (30 meters).

Posture: Unlike most modern reptiles, dinosaurs walked with their legs positioned directly beneath their bodies (similar to mammals), giving them more efficient movement. This allowed many dinosaurs to become large and fast-moving.

Skulls and Teeth: Dinosaur skulls varied greatly depending on diet:

Carnivores (meat-eaters) had sharp, serrated teeth for tearing flesh (*Tyrannosaurus rex*, *Velociraptor*).

Herbivores (plant-eaters) had flat, grinding teeth or specialized beaks for eating plants (*Triceratops*, *Stegosaurus*).

Feathers: Many theropod dinosaurs had feathers, particularly smaller species. Evidence suggests that feathers might have been used for insulation, display, or even flight (in the case of bird-like dinosaurs).

Habitat:

Dinosaurs lived in nearly every type of environment on Earth, including forests, deserts, plains, and swamps. Fossil evidence suggests they inhabited every continent, including Antarctica.

Diet:

Dinosaurs were diverse in their diets:

Carnivores (like *Allosaurus* and *T. rex*) hunted other animals for food.

Herbivores (like *Diplodocus* and *Stegosaurus*) fed on a variety of plants, from ferns and cycads to conifers and flowering plants.

Some dinosaurs, like **omnivores** (potentially *Oviraptor*), may have had a more varied diet that included plants, eggs, and small animals.

Reproduction:

Dinosaurs laid **eggs**. Fossilized dinosaur eggs and nests have been found, showing that some dinosaurs cared for their young after they hatched, similar to modern birds.

Some species nested in colonies, with many individuals laying their eggs in the same area.

Types of Dinosaurs

Theropods (Carnivorous Dinosaurs):

These were **bipedal**, meaning they walked on two legs.

Famous examples include *Tyrannosaurus rex*, *Velociraptor*, and *Spinosaurus*.

Theropods ranged in size from small, bird-like species to the largest land carnivores ever known.

Sauropods (Long-Necked Herbivores):

Sauropods were among the **largest animals** to have ever lived on land.

Examples include *Brachiosaurus*, *Apatosaurus*, and *Diplodocus*.

They had long necks and tails, small heads, and massive, pillar-like legs.

Ornithopods (Duck-Billed Dinosaurs):

Ornithopods were bipedal or quadrupedal herbivores.

The most famous of this group is *Hadrosaurus*, known for its **duck-billed** mouth, used to strip leaves and plants.

Some species had crests on their heads, which may have been used for communication.

<u>Ceratopsians</u> (Horned Dinosaurs):

These were quadrupedal herbivores known for their **frills** and **facial horns**.

Triceratops is the most well-known ceratopsian, with its large frill and three facial horns.

<u>Stegosaurs</u> (Plated Dinosaurs):

Stegosaurus is the most famous example of this group, known for the **bony plates** along its back and **spiked tail**.

They were quadrupedal herbivores with relatively small brains compared to their body size.

<u>Ankylosaurs</u> (Armored Dinosaurs):

These dinosaurs had **heavily armored bodies** with bony plates and often a **clubbed tail** for defense.

Ankylosaurus is a well-known member of this group.

Extinction

Dinosaurs, along with many other species, went extinct around **66 million years ago** during the **Cretaceous-Paleogene (K-Pg) extinction event**. The most widely accepted theory is that a **massive asteroid** or comet struck the Earth, creating the **Chicxulub crater** in Mexico. This impact caused massive fires, tsunamis, and climate changes that led to the extinction of around **75% of all species**, including most dinosaurs.

However, some small, feathered theropods survived and eventually evolved into modern **birds**, making them the direct descendants of dinosaurs.

Importance of Dinosaurs

Dinosaurs are crucial to understanding the **evolution of life on Earth** and the dynamics of ancient ecosystems.

They provide insights into adaptation, survival, and extinction, with lessons that extend to the study of modern animals and environmental changes.

Dinosaurs have captured the public's imagination for generations, sparking interest in **paleontology** and leading to major scientific discoveries.

Dinosaurs were a diverse and successful group of reptiles that dominated the Earth for millions of years. They ranged in size, shape, diet, and behavior, filling numerous ecological roles. Although they went extinct in the Cretaceous-Paleogene event, their legacy lives on through modern birds, which are their closest living relatives. Paleontologists continue to discover new species and learn more about the life, behavior, and extinction of these incredible creatures.

The Extinction Of Dinosaurs

The extinction of dinosaurs is one of the most significant events in Earth's history. It happened approximately 66 million years ago at the end of the Cretaceous period. Scientists believe that the extinction was caused by a combination of catastrophic events, but the leading theory is the impact of a massive asteroid. **Here's a detailed explanation:**

Asteroid Impact Theory

The most widely accepted theory is that a giant asteroid, estimated to be about 6 to 10 miles (10 to 15 km) in diameter, struck the Earth near what is now the Yucatán Peninsula in Mexico. The impact site, called the Chicxulub crater, is buried under the Gulf of Mexico.

Immediate Effects of the Impact

Shockwaves and Tsunamis: The asteroid struck with incredible force, releasing more energy than a billion nuclear bombs. The initial impact caused massive shock waves and tsunamis that affected coastlines worldwide.

Massive Fires: The heat from the impact likely caused widespread wildfires. Debris and vaporized material were ejected into the atmosphere, and this material rained down on Earth, igniting fires over large areas of land.

Global Consequences

Debris in the Atmosphere: The impact blasted dust, ash, and sulfur gases into the atmosphere, creating a thick cloud that blocked sunlight. This drastically reduced temperatures, a phenomenon often referred to as an "impact winter."

Climate Change: With sunlight blocked for months or even years, photosynthesis in plants stopped, leading to the collapse of the food chain. Temperatures dropped, and a "nuclear winter" scenario unfolded, making it nearly impossible for life to survive in many regions.

Acid Rain: The sulfur gases released by the impact may have combined with water in the atmosphere, producing acid rain, which further damaged plant life and the environment.

Volcanic Activity (Deccan Traps)

Around the same time as the asteroid impact, there was significant volcanic activity in what is now India, known as the Deccan Traps. These volcanic eruptions released massive amounts of lava and gases, including sulfur dioxide and carbon dioxide.

Lava Flows: The lava from these eruptions covered vast areas, altering the landscape.

Climate Effects: The volcanic gases likely contributed to global climate change. Sulfur dioxide in the atmosphere could have caused cooling (similar to the impact of winter), while carbon dioxide would have contributed to global warming after the dust settled.

Ocean Acidification: The release of gases like sulfur and carbon dioxide may have also acidified the oceans, harming marine life.

Combination of Factors

The combination of the asteroid impact and volcanic activity likely created a perfect storm of catastrophic events that led to the mass extinction. While the asteroid impact caused immediate destruction, the volcanic eruptions might have worsened the long-term environmental effects.

Who Survived?

Although dinosaurs went extinct, not all life forms were wiped out. Small animals like mammals, birds (which are descendants of certain dinosaurs), reptiles, amphibians, and some fish survived. These animals were smaller and could adapt to the changing environment, finding shelter or food more easily than the large dinosaurs.

Why Dinosaurs Went Extinct

Dinosaurs were large and dependent on specific environments for food and survival. When their food sources (like plants) died off due to lack of sunlight and harsh climates, it was difficult for these large creatures to find enough to eat. Furthermore, their larger size may have made them less adaptable to the rapid environmental changes caused by the asteroid impact and volcanic activity.

The Evidence

Scientists have gathered strong evidence to support this theory:

Chicxulub Crater: The impact site in Mexico matches the timeline of the extinction.

Iridium Layer: Around the world, a thin layer of rock rich in iridium (a rare element often found in asteroids) has been discovered at the boundary between the Cretaceous and Paleogene periods. This is known as the K-Pg boundary.

Fossil Record: Dinosaur fossils suddenly disappear after this boundary, marking the end of their dominance on Earth.

The extinction of dinosaurs was likely caused by the catastrophic impact of a massive asteroid, which triggered fires, blocked sunlight, and caused a global winter. This, combined with volcanic activity, resulted in a drastic change in the Earth's climate and environment, leading to the extinction of about 75% of all species, including the dinosaurs. Smaller, adaptable species like mammals and birds survived, allowing life to eventually recover and evolve.

Chicxulub crater

The **Chicxulub crater** is a massive impact crater located on the **Yucatán Peninsula** in **Mexico**. It was formed around **66 million years ago** when a **huge asteroid** or comet, about **6 to 10 miles (10 to 15 kilometers)** in diameter, struck the Earth. This impact is strongly linked to the **Cretaceous-Paleogene (K-Pg) extinction event**, which caused the extinction of about **75% of Earth's species**, including all non-avian dinosaurs.

Key Features of the Chicxulub Crater

Size:

The crater is about **93 miles (150 kilometers)** in diameter and **12 miles (20 kilometers)** deep, making it one of the largest known impact craters on Earth.

The impact released energy equivalent to billions of atomic bombs, creating devastating effects worldwide.

Location:

The crater is mostly buried under the **Gulf of Mexico**, with parts of it extending onto the Yucatán Peninsula.

Its location was discovered in the **late 1970s** by geologists looking for oil. They noticed a ring-like structure beneath the surface, which was later identified as the Chicxulub crater.

Impact and Consequences:

The asteroid impact had immediate and far-reaching effects. It caused massive shockwaves, fires, tsunamis, and a huge release of vaporized rock and debris into the atmosphere.

This debris blocked sunlight for months or even years, leading to a dramatic cooling of the Earth's climate, a phenomenon known as an "impact winter."

The lack of sunlight caused the collapse of the food chain, as plants and phytoplankton (the base of most ecosystems) could no longer photosynthesize.

Acid rain and other environmental effects further disrupted life on Earth, contributing to the mass extinction.

Discovery of the Crater's Role in Dinosaur Extinction:

In the **1980s**, scientists found a worldwide layer of rock enriched with **iridium**, a rare element more common in asteroids than in Earth's crust. This layer, known as the **K-Pg boundary**, coincided with the time of the mass extinction.

The discovery of the Chicxulub crater in the 1990s, along with its age and the presence of shocked quartz (a mineral deformed by intense pressure), provided strong evidence linking the crater to the extinction event.

Global Impact of the Chicxulub Event

Tsunamis and Fires:

The impact likely triggered massive tsunamis that affected coastlines far from the impact site.

Heat from the impact ignited wildfires across large areas of land.

Atmospheric Changes:

Dust, ash, and sulfur gases from the impact were thrown high into the atmosphere, blocking sunlight and causing a "nuclear winter" effect.

Temperatures dropped drastically, and the sudden cooling may have persisted for years, making it difficult for life to survive.

Mass Extinction:

The aftermath of the Chicxulub impact is considered the primary cause of the **Cretaceous-Paleogene (K-Pg) extinction event**, which wiped out not only the non-avian dinosaurs but also many marine and terrestrial species, including some plants and microorganisms.

Significance of the Chicxulub Crater

The Chicxulub crater is one of the most important geological sites because it provides direct evidence of how catastrophic asteroid impacts can cause mass extinctions. It helps scientists understand Earth's history, the fragility of life, and how sudden, dramatic events can reshape ecosystems and species.

The **Chicxulub crater** marks the site of one of Earth's most cataclysmic events: the asteroid impact that contributed to the extinction of the dinosaurs. Its discovery has been crucial in explaining the mass extinction 66 million years ago and the role such impacts have played in shaping the course of life on Earth.

Therizinosaurus

Therizinosaurus was a large, unusual herbivorous dinosaur that lived during the **Late Cretaceous period**, about **70 million years ago**, in what is now **Mongolia**. It is known for its unique features, particularly its gigantic claws. Although Therizinosaurus was initially a mystery to paleontologists, further discoveries have provided a clearer picture of this remarkable dinosaur.

Key Characteristics of Therizinosaurus

Gigantic Claws:

The most striking feature of Therizinosaurus is its **enormous claws**, which could grow up to **3 feet (1 meter)** in length. These are the longest claws of any known dinosaur.

Despite their terrifying appearance, these claws were likely used for tasks like **pulling down branches** to feed on leaves and possibly for defense.

Herbivorous Diet:

Therizinosaurus belonged to a group of dinosaurs known as **theropods**, which typically included carnivores like **Tyrannosaurus rex**. However, Therizinosaurus was a plant-eater.

It likely fed on leaves, fruits, and other vegetation, using its long neck and claws to reach high branches in the forests where it lived.

Body Structure:

Therizinosaurus was a **large dinosaur**, with an estimated length of about **33 feet (10 meters)** and weighing around **5 tons**.

It had a long neck, small head, a large belly, and a bipedal posture, meaning it walked on two legs.

Its body was bulky, allowing it to process large amounts of plant matter.

Feathers:

Although direct evidence of feathers in Therizinosaurus hasn't been found, related dinosaurs in the same family (the **Therizinosauridae**) had **feathers**, so it is likely that Therizinosaurus had some form of feathery covering.

Theropod Anomaly:

Despite being a theropod, which is the same group that includes famous meat-eaters like **Velociraptor** and **Allosaurus**, Therizinosaurus was **herbivorous**. This makes it a notable exception to the typically carnivorous nature of theropods.

Discovery and Classification

Therizinosaurus was first discovered in the **1940s** in Mongolia. Its name means **"scythe lizard,"** referring to its large, scythe-like claws.

Initially, due to its strange claws, paleontologists thought it might have been a large **turtle-like creature**. However, later findings revealed that it was indeed a dinosaur and part of the theropod group.

Function of the Claws

The true function of Therizinosaurus' claws is still debated, but some possible uses include:

Foraging: To pull down branches and strip leaves from plants.

Defense: The claws could have been used to defend against predators.

Mating Displays: The claws may have also played a role in social behavior, such as attracting mates.

Therizinosaurus was a remarkable and unique dinosaur with long claws, a plant-eating diet, and a body structure that set it apart from most theropods. It lived in what is now Mongolia and was likely covered in feathers. Despite its fearsome appearance, it was likely a peaceful herbivore, using its impressive claws for feeding and perhaps defense.

Dinosaur Known For Having 500 Teeth

The dinosaur known for having around 500 teeth is the Nigersaurus. It was a herbivorous dinosaur that lived approximately 110 million years ago during the Middle Cretaceous period. **Here's some key information about Nigersaurus:**

Key Characteristics of Nigersaurus:

Teeth: Nigersaurus had a highly unusual skull with a wide, flat mouth lined with around 500 teeth, arranged in rows. Its teeth were specialized for grazing low-lying plants like ferns and horsetails.

The teeth were constantly being replaced. Each tooth had a "backup" tooth ready to replace it once it wore out, allowing Nigersaurus to keep a continuous supply of fresh teeth for its grazing diet.

Size: Nigersaurus was relatively small for a sauropod. It was about 30 feet (9 meters) long, with a lightweight build compared to other giant sauropods.

Habitat: It lived in what is now Niger in Africa, in a region that was once lush and filled with vegetation. The fossils of Nigersaurus were first discovered in the Sahara Desert.

Skull: Its skull was light and thin, with large openings that made it unique among sauropods. The mouth was wide, and the teeth were arranged in a sort of "vacuum cleaner" configuration, perfect for sweeping up plants from the ground.

Nigersaurus is famous for its remarkable dental structure, with around 500 teeth designed for continuous replacement. This fascinating dinosaur had a specialized diet and an extraordinary set of adaptations for grazing on low-lying vegetation.

First Dinosaurs To Get Extinct

The extinction of dinosaurs occurred during the Cretaceous-Paleogene (K-Pg) extinction event around 66 million years ago, but it didn't happen all at once. Different dinosaur species may have gone extinct at varying rates, with some dying out before the final mass extinction due to gradual environmental changes. However, pinpointing the exact "first" dinosaurs to go extinct is difficult because extinction patterns are complex and often drawn out over time.

Key Points in Understanding Early Extinction

Gradual Decline: Some groups of dinosaurs started declining even before the asteroid impact due to changes in climate, sea levels, and vegetation.

Environmental Stresses: Dinosaurs that were more sensitive to environmental changes may have been the first to disappear as their habitats altered.

Dinosaurs Likely to Have Gone Extinct First

Sauropods (Long-necked dinosaurs)

Examples: *Apatosaurus, Brachiosaurus, Diplodocus.*

Sauropods were large herbivores and relied on vast quantities of vegetation. As plant life started to change due to climate shifts and volcanic activity, their food sources may have dwindled, making them more vulnerable to early extinction.

Fossil evidence suggests that some sauropod species began to decline by the Late Cretaceous, though others survived until the asteroid impact.

Stegosaurs

Examples: *Stegosaurus.*

Stegosaurs, famous for their bony plates and spikes, were already in decline by the end of the Jurassic period (about 150 million years ago), long before the asteroid impact. Most stegosaurs were extinct before the final mass extinction event, making them one of the earlier groups of dinosaurs to disappear.

Ankylosaurs (Armored dinosaurs)

Examples: *Ankylosaurus, Euoplocephalus.*

Ankylosaurs were heavily armored dinosaurs with clubbed tails. Fossil records indicate that some ankylosaur species disappeared before the mass extinction, while others survived up until the very end. Their slow-moving nature may have made it harder for them to adapt to rapidly changing environments.

Ornithopods (Duck-billed dinosaurs)

Examples: *Iguanodon, Hadrosaurus.*

Ornithopods were among the most common herbivores in the Late Cretaceous. While some species survived until the final extinction, fossil evidence suggests that certain species began to disappear earlier, possibly due to habitat changes.

Gradual Extinctions Before the Asteroid Impact

The extinction event that wiped out the dinosaurs wasn't entirely sudden for all species. **Some dinosaurs were already in decline due to:**

Volcanic activity: The Deccan Traps eruptions in India may have caused gradual climate changes, making survival harder for certain species.

Sea level changes: Shifting sea levels altered habitats, causing some coastal and inland environments to disappear.

Competition for food: Changes in vegetation and the appearance of new plant species might have disrupted food sources for some dinosaurs.

Who Survived Until the Very End?

The theropods, which included meat-eating dinosaurs like Tyrannosaurus rex and small feathered dinosaurs, were among the last to survive. Some of these small theropods are believed to be the ancestors of modern birds.

Ceratopsians, such as Triceratops, and other horned dinosaurs were still thriving just before the mass extinction.

The first dinosaurs to go extinct were likely those that were less adaptable to changing environments, such as stegosaurus (which disappeared much earlier) and some species of sauropods and ankylosaurs. Environmental changes before the asteroid impact, such as volcanic activity and climate shifts, contributed to the gradual decline of certain groups of dinosaurs. However, the final mass extinction event rapidly wiped out most dinosaur species, regardless of their previous resilience.

Most Dangerous Dinosaur

The title of the "most dangerous dinosaur" is often debated among paleontologists and enthusiasts, as different dinosaurs exhibited different traits that made them fearsome predators or effective defenders. However, certain species are frequently highlighted as among the most dangerous due to their physical abilities, size, strength, and hunting tactics. **Here are some of the leading candidates for the most dangerous dinosaurs, along with detailed explanations of what made each of them formidable.**

Tyrannosaurus rex (T. rex)

Overview:

Time Period: Late Cretaceous Period (~68–66 million years ago)

Size: Around 40 feet (12 meters) in length and up to 12 feet (3.66 meters) tall at the hips

Weight: Up to 9 tons

Diet: Carnivorous

Why It Was Dangerous:

Bite Force: *Tyrannosaurus rex* had one of the most powerful bites of any land animal ever discovered. Its bite force has been estimated to be as much as 12,800 pounds (5,800 kg) per square inch, capable of crushing bone. This allowed it to easily dispatch prey or scavenge by crushing bones to get at marrow.

Teeth: The T. rex had serrated, banana-shaped teeth about 12 inches long, which were designed to tear through flesh and break bones.

Speed and Agility: Despite its large size, some scientists believe T. rex could run at speeds of 20–25 mph (32–40 km/h), though there is debate over whether it was primarily a fast-moving predator or a slower-moving scavenger.

Senses: T. rex had highly developed senses of smell and vision. Fossil evidence suggests it had binocular vision, giving it depth perception and making it an excellent hunter.

Hunting Strategy: Some paleontologists believe T. rex may have hunted in groups, potentially making it even more dangerous in pack hunts.

Spinosaurus

Overview:

Time Period: Late Cretaceous (~100–93 million years ago)

Size: 50–60 feet (15–18 meters) long

Weight: 7 to 9 tons

Diet: Carnivorous, primarily fish-eating (piscivorous), but it could hunt terrestrial prey as well.

Why It Was Dangerous:

Size: *Spinosaurus* is considered the largest predatory dinosaur, even bigger than T. rex. Its size alone would have made it an intimidating predator.

Adaptation for Water: *Spinosaurus* was semi-aquatic, living both on land and in water. It had a crocodile-like snout, which was effective for catching fish. Fossil evidence suggests it hunted large fish and possibly small or medium-sized dinosaurs near water sources.

Sail: The sail on its back, formed by elongated spines, may have been used for display, thermoregulation, or even intimidation.

Claws: *Spinosaurus* had large, powerful arms equipped with sharp claws, which may have been used for slashing prey. Its claws made it dangerous both in water and on land.

Giganotosaurus

Overview:

Time Period: Late Cretaceous (~99.6–97 million years ago)

Size: 40–43 feet (12–13 meters) long

Weight: 8 tons

Diet: Carnivorous

Why It Was Dangerous:

Size: *Giganotosaurus* was one of the largest theropods and potentially rivaled T. rex in terms of size.

Speed: It is believed to have been faster than T. rex, possibly reaching speeds of 20–30 mph (32–48 km/h), allowing it to chase down large prey.

Brain and Hunting Behavior: Although its brain was relatively small, *Giganotosaurus* might have hunted in packs, like modern-day wolves, to take down large herbivores such as the giant Argentinosaurus (one of the largest land animals ever).

Bite and Teeth: Its bite, though not as powerful as T. rex's, was still formidable, with sharp teeth designed for slicing flesh rather than crushing bone.

Utahraptor

Overview:

Time Period: Early Cretaceous (~126 million years ago)

Size: 20 feet (6 meters) long

Weight: 1,100 to 1,500 pounds (500–700 kg)

Diet: Carnivorous

Why It Was Dangerous:

Agility: *Utahraptor* was a fast, agile predator that could use its speed to outmaneuver prey.

Claws: It had a sickle-shaped claw on each foot, about 9 inches long, which could be used to slash or stab prey. This made *Utahraptor* particularly lethal in close-quarters combat.

Intelligence: Raptors, including *Utahraptor*, were believed to be relatively intelligent for dinosaurs. They may have used pack hunting strategies to take down much larger prey.

Feathers: Though direct evidence of feathers in *Utahraptor* has not been found, many theropods in the raptor family are now believed to have had feathers, which might have helped with balance, display, or warmth.

Velociraptor

Overview:

Time Period: Late Cretaceous (~75–71 million years ago)

Size: 6.8 feet (2 meters) long

Weight: 33 pounds (15 kg)

Diet: Carnivorous

Why It Was Dangerous:

Pack Hunter: *Velociraptor* is often portrayed as a deadly pack hunter. Though small, it could overwhelm prey using teamwork.

Claws: Like *Utahraptor*, it had a retractable sickle-shaped claw on each foot that was used for slashing and stabbing prey.

Speed and Agility: *Velociraptor* was lightweight and fast, with the ability to chase down smaller prey or escape larger predators.

Intelligence: It is thought to have been relatively smart compared to other dinosaurs, possibly using coordinated pack attacks, although this behavior is mostly speculative based on fossil evidence.

Allosaurus

Overview:

Time Period: Late Jurassic (~155–150 million years ago)

Size: 28–39 feet (8.5–12 meters) long

Weight: 1.5 to 4.5 tons

Diet: Carnivorous

Why It Was Dangerous:

Bite and Hunting: *Allosaurus* had strong, sharp teeth, and it is believed to have used a "hatchet" style of hunting, where it would slash at prey with its jaws, inflicting deep wounds.

Group Hunting: There is some evidence to suggest that *Allosaurus* may have hunted in groups, which would have made it a more formidable predator, especially against large herbivores like *Stegosaurus* or *Apatosaurus*.

Agility: For its size, *Allosaurus* was relatively agile and may have been capable of quick, powerful movements to take down prey.

Determining the "most dangerous" dinosaur depends on various factors, such as size, speed, intelligence, hunting techniques, and physical weapons like teeth and claws. Tyrannosaurus rex is often considered the most dangerous due to its size, strength, and powerful bite. However, Spinosaurus could have been more dangerous in aquatic environments, and raptors like Utahraptor and Velociraptor were smaller but deadly due to their speed, agility, and likely pack-hunting behavior.

Each of these dinosaurs was incredibly well-adapted to its environment and time, making them formidable predators in their own right.

Calmest Dinosaur

The "calmest" dinosaur is difficult to determine with certainty because behavioral characteristics like calmness are not easily preserved in fossils. However, certain dinosaurs are believed to have been **herbivores** that primarily spent their time foraging for food and defending themselves from predators, rather than being active hunters. These dinosaurs might be considered more **docile** or "calm" compared to aggressive predators. Some large herbivores, due to their size and relative lack of predators, may have had a more relaxed lifestyle. Below are some examples of dinosaurs that are often thought to have been calm, along with explanations.

Sauropods (Long-Necked Herbivores)

Overview:

Time Period: Jurassic to Cretaceous Period

Examples: *Apatosaurus, Diplodocus, Brachiosaurus, Argentinosaurus*

Size: Among the largest animals ever to walk the Earth; could grow up to 100 feet (30 meters) long and weigh up to 100 tons.

Diet: Herbivorous, feeding mainly on high-growing plants like conifers and cycads.

Why They Were Likely Calm:

Size as a Defense: Sauropods, due to their massive size, had very few natural predators as adults. Predators like *Allosaurus* or *Tyrannosaurus rex* would have had difficulty bringing down such large animals. As a result, they likely didn't need to be particularly aggressive.

Behavior: These dinosaurs likely spent most of their day moving slowly and steadily, browsing on vegetation, and using their long necks to reach food that was out of reach for other herbivores. They may have lived in herds, which offered additional protection, reducing the need for constant vigilance or stress.

Limb Structure: Their pillar-like legs were designed for supporting large weight, not for running or quick movements. This suggests they led relatively slow-paced lives.

Defensive Traits: Although they were calm, they could defend themselves if needed. Some sauropods, like *Diplodocus*, had long, whip-like tails that could be used for defense against predators.

Stegosaurus

Overview:

Time Period: Late Jurassic (~155–150 million years ago)

Size: Up to 30 feet (9 meters) long and weighed around 5–7 tons.

Diet: Herbivorous, feeding on low-growing plants and ferns.

Why It Was Likely Calm:

Defense Over Aggression: *Stegosaurus* had defensive adaptations, like large, bony plates along its back and a spiked tail (called a **thagomizer**), which it could swing to defend itself. However, it wasn't a fast or agile dinosaur, so it likely relied on these passive defenses rather than aggressive behavior.

Low Feeding Activity: *Stegosaurus* fed on low-growing plants, suggesting it spent much of its day grazing rather than actively seeking out food or engaging in stressful activities.

Brain and Behavior: Its brain was relatively small compared to its body size, leading some scientists to hypothesize that *Stegosaurus* may have had a more instinct-driven and less complex behavior, which might suggest a simple, calm existence focused on eating and survival rather than active interaction with its environment.

Ankylosaurus

Overview:

Time Period: Late Cretaceous (~68–66 million years ago)

Size: 20–30 feet (6–9 meters) long and weighed up to 6 tons.

Diet: Herbivorous, feeding on low-lying plants.

Why It Was Likely Calm:

Defensive Armor: *Ankylosaurus* had a body covered in **thick bony armor** plates and a large, club-like tail, which it could use to defend itself from predators like *Tyrannosaurus rex*. This armor made it well-protected from attacks, so it likely didn't need to be particularly aggressive or fearful. Its best defense was to stay still and let its armor do the work.

Slow-Moving: Its stocky build and armor plating meant *Ankylosaurus* wasn't built for speed. It likely moved slowly through its environment, foraging on low-lying vegetation. Its primary focus would have been on grazing and maintaining its defenses rather than being an active predator.

Peaceful Browsing: Like other herbivores, it likely spent most of its time calmly grazing on plants rather than engaging in confrontations.

Triceratops

Overview:

Time Period: Late Cretaceous (~68–66 million years ago)

Size: Up to 30 feet (9 meters) long and weighed around 6–12 tons.

Diet: Herbivorous, feeding on cycads, ferns, and other low-growing plants.

Why It Was Likely Calm:

Passive Nature: *Triceratops* is often depicted as a relatively calm herbivore that spent most of its time grazing. Its large, frilled skull and **three facial horns** were primarily defensive features, used to protect itself from predators like *Tyrannosaurus rex* rather than for attacking other animals.

Defense Over Aggression: While it could defend itself effectively with its horns, *Triceratops* likely preferred to avoid confrontations unless provoked. Fossil evidence of injuries suggests it may have engaged in combat with predators or other *Triceratops*, but it would have been more focused on survival than on seeking fights.

Herd Behavior: *Triceratops* may have lived in herds, which would have provided additional protection from predators. Herding animals often exhibit calmer, more social behavior when not threatened.

Iguanodon

Overview:

Time Period: Early Cretaceous (~140–120 million years ago)

Size: Around 30 feet (9 meters) long and weighed up to 5 tons.

Diet: Herbivorous, feeding on cycads, conifers, and other plants.

Why It Was Likely Calm:

Adaptable Herbivore: *Iguanodon* was one of the first dinosaurs to be discovered and named, and it was an herbivore that fed on a wide range of plants. Its beak was used to crop vegetation, while its grinding teeth helped it process tough plant material.

Thumb Spike: It had a large **thumb spike**, which could be used for defense, but it wasn't an aggressive animal. This spike was likely a last-resort weapon against predators, suggesting it relied more on passive defenses.

Social Behavior: Evidence suggests that *Iguanodon* may have lived in herds, a behavior common among herbivores. Herding behavior typically reduces individual stress and provides safety in numbers, allowing these animals to live relatively peaceful lives.

General Characteristics of Calm Dinosaurs:

Herbivorous Lifestyle: Most of the dinosaurs considered calm were herbivores. Their lives were largely spent foraging for plants, which doesn't require the same aggression or energy as hunting.

Large Size or Defensive Traits: Dinosaurs like sauropods, *Ankylosaurus*, and *Triceratops* had natural defenses—size, armor, or horns—that allowed them to avoid confrontation rather than seek it. Their physical traits made them more defensive than aggressive.

Herding Behavior: Many herbivorous dinosaurs lived in herds, which provided protection from predators and allowed them to focus on feeding and socializing rather than constant vigilance or aggression.

Slow Movements: Calm dinosaurs, particularly large herbivores, tended to move slowly and deliberately, focusing on conserving energy for their large bodies rather than engaging in fast-paced, high-stress activities.

The calmest dinosaurs were likely large, herbivorous species such as **sauropods** (*Apatosaurus*, *Brachiosaurus*), **armored dinosaurs** (*Ankylosaurus*), and possibly even **ceratopsians** like *Triceratops*. These dinosaurs, due to their size, defense mechanisms, or herd behaviors, lived relatively peaceful lives, spending much of their time grazing or moving slowly through their environment. While they could defend themselves if necessary, their primary focus was likely on feeding and survival rather than aggression or conflict.

Dinosaur Eggs

Dinosaurs, like modern birds and reptiles, are believed to have laid eggs rather than giving live birth. **Here's a detailed explanation of how dinosaurs reproduced and raised their offspring:**

Egg Laying

Nesting Behavior: Most dinosaurs are thought to have laid eggs in nests. Evidence from fossilized nests and eggs suggests that some dinosaurs created nests by digging in the ground, while others might have used vegetation to build a safe area for their eggs.

Egg Types: Dinosaur eggs varied in size, shape, and texture depending on the species. Some were round, while others were elongated, and some had hard, mineralized shells, while others were softer and leathery.

Clutch Size

Number of Eggs: The number of eggs in a clutch (the group of eggs laid at one time) varied widely among species. Some dinosaurs, like the small theropods, might have laid just a few eggs, while larger dinosaurs, such as sauropods, could lay dozens of eggs in a single nesting attempt.

Incubation

Temperature Regulation: While it is not definitively known how dinosaurs incubated their eggs, some theories suggest they might have used external heat sources (like the sun) or possibly even body heat, similar to how modern birds and reptiles do.

Brooding Behavior: Some evidence suggests that certain dinosaurs, especially theropods (which are closely related to modern birds), might have exhibited parental care, such as brooding over their eggs to keep them warm.

Hatching

Hatching Process: After a period of incubation, baby dinosaurs (called hatchlings) would emerge from their eggs. Fossils of hatchlings indicate that they were often much smaller than their adult counterparts.

Development: Newly hatched dinosaurs likely had to fend for themselves immediately after hatching. However, some species might have received care from their parents, helping them find food and avoid predators.

Growth and Development

Juvenile Stages: Once hatched, baby dinosaurs would go through several growth stages. The rate of growth varied among species, with some growing rapidly and reaching maturity within a few years, while others took much longer.

Behavioral Differences: Juvenile dinosaurs may have exhibited different behaviors compared to adults, such as being more agile and relying on speed to escape from predators.

Parental Care

Evidence of Care: Fossil evidence suggests that some dinosaurs exhibited signs of parental care. For example, nests with multiple eggs or nests containing both adult and juvenile fossils indicate that some species might have cared for their young after they hatched.

Examples: Species like *Oviraptor* and *Troodon* are often cited as dinosaurs that might have shown parental care due to fossil evidence showing adults near nests.

Dinosaurs reproduced by laying eggs, which they often nested in safe locations. The eggs varied in size and number depending on the species. After hatching, baby dinosaurs could be independent or receive some parental care, depending on the species. The growth rates and development of young dinosaurs varied widely, influencing their survival and adaptability in their environments.

Misconceptions About Dinosaurs

There are many misconceptions about dinosaurs that have persisted over the years. **Here are some common mistakes people often make:**

Dinosaurs Were All Giant Monsters

Reality: While many dinosaurs were large, not all were gigantic. There were many small dinosaurs, some of which were the size of chickens or even smaller. For example, *Microraptor* was a small, feathered dinosaur that was about the size of a crow.

Dinosaurs and Humans Coexisted

Reality: Dinosaurs went extinct approximately 65 million years ago, long before humans appeared on Earth. The earliest ancestors of humans appeared millions of years after the last non-avian dinosaurs died out.

Dinosaurs Were Cold-Blooded Like Modern Reptiles

Reality: Recent research suggests that many dinosaurs were likely warm-blooded (endothermic), similar to modern birds. Some species exhibited features like feathers, which are typically associated with warm-blooded animals, indicating a more complex metabolism.

All Dinosaurs Were Slow and Clumsy

Reality: While some large dinosaurs like sauropods were indeed slow-moving, many theropods, such as *Velociraptor*, were agile and fast. Some species could run at impressive speeds to catch prey or evade predators.

Dinosaurs Were Just Like Modern Reptiles

Reality: While dinosaurs share a common ancestor with modern reptiles, they were a distinct group with many unique adaptations. For instance, some dinosaurs had feathers, complex social behaviors, and advanced parenting strategies that are not found in most modern reptiles.

Tyrannosaurus rex Was the Largest Predator

Reality: Although *Tyrannosaurus rex* is one of the most famous large predators, it was not the largest. Other theropods, like *Spinosaurus*, were larger in size and weight. *T. rex* was among the top predators of its time but not the largest.

Dinosaurs Went Extinct Because of a Single Event

Reality: While the Chicxulub impactor (asteroid) is often cited as a primary cause of the mass extinction event that ended the non-avian dinosaurs, other factors also contributed, including volcanic activity, climate change, and sea level fluctuations.

Dinosaurs Were Not Social Animals

Reality: Evidence suggests that many dinosaur species were social and lived in groups or herds. Fossil discoveries, such as nests and tracks, indicate cooperative behaviors and social structures among some dinosaur species.

Dinosaurs Were All Carnivorous

Reality: Dinosaurs had a wide range of diets. While some were carnivorous (like *Tyrannosaurus rex*), many were herbivorous (like *Brachiosaurus*), and some were omnivorous, eating both plants and animals (like *Iguanodon*).

Dinosaurs Were Covered in Scales

Reality: While many dinosaurs had scaly skin, evidence shows that some, especially theropods, had feathers or feather-like structures. This suggests a greater diversity in skin coverings than previously thought.

These misconceptions highlight how our understanding of dinosaurs has evolved over time with new discoveries and research. While popular culture often portrays dinosaurs in simplified or exaggerated ways, ongoing paleontological studies continue to reveal a more nuanced picture of these fascinating creatures.

Nigersaurus (The Dinosaur With 500 Teeth)

More Detail:

Nigersaurus is a genus of dinosaur that lived during the Late Cretaceous period, around 115 to 105 million years ago. **Here are some key details about this fascinating dinosaur:**

Classification

Type: *Nigersaurus* is classified as a sauropod, which is a group of large, long-necked herbivorous dinosaurs.

Family: It belongs to the family Rebbachisauridae, known for their distinctive long necks and relatively short tails.

Discovery

Fossil Location: The first fossils of *Nigersaurus* were discovered in Niger, Africa, in the 1970s. The dinosaur was named in 1999.

Fossil Characteristics: Fossils include a partial skeleton, which provided important insights into its physical features and lifestyle.

Physical Characteristics

Size: *Nigersaurus* was relatively small compared to other sauropods, measuring about 30 to 36 feet (9 to 11 meters) in length.

Unique Skull: It had a long, wide skull with an unusual set of hundreds of replacement teeth, specifically adapted for grazing. It is estimated to have had up to 500 teeth.

Cranial Features: The skull's shape and teeth suggest it was well-adapted for browsing low-lying vegetation, similar to modern-day herbivores like cows.

Diet and Behavior

Herbivorous: *Nigersaurus* primarily fed on soft plants, including ferns and other low-lying vegetation, thanks to its specialized teeth and jaw structure.

Feeding Method: Its long neck allowed it to reach down to the ground to graze efficiently.

Habitat

Environment: *Nigersaurus* lived in a semi-arid environment with a variety of plants. Fossil evidence suggests it inhabited floodplains and regions with abundant plant life.

Paleontological Significance

Nigersaurus is significant because it provides insights into the diversity of sauropods in Africa and their adaptations to specific ecological niches. Its unique feeding adaptations and skull structure help scientists understand how different dinosaurs evolved to exploit various food sources.

Nigersaurus is a fascinating sauropod dinosaur known for its unique skull structure, large number of teeth, and herbivorous diet. Its discovery has contributed to our understanding of dinosaur diversity and adaptation during the Late Cretaceous period.

Dinosaur Bones

Dinosaur bones are fascinating subjects of study that provide valuable insights into the biology, behavior, and evolution of these ancient creatures. Here are some detailed facts about dinosaur bones:

Composition

Bone Structure: Dinosaur bones are made primarily of a mineralized matrix that includes collagen (a protein) and hydroxyapatite (a mineral form of calcium phosphate). This structure gives bones their strength and rigidity.

Porosity: Dinosaur bones can vary in porosity. Some bones were dense and strong, while others were more porous, indicating different functional adaptations. For example, the bones of some large dinosaurs were hollow to reduce weight.

Growth Rings

Annual Growth Rings: Like trees, dinosaur bones can exhibit growth rings that indicate age. These rings can provide insights into the growth rates of dinosaurs and their life histories. For instance, some studies suggest that certain dinosaurs, like *Allosaurus*, had growth patterns similar to modern reptiles, growing quickly during their early years and then slowing down.

Seasonal Growth: Growth rings may also indicate seasonal changes, suggesting that dinosaurs experienced periods of rapid growth during favorable conditions (e.g., abundant food) and slower growth during harsher seasons.

Fossilization Process

Fossilization: Dinosaur bones become fossils through a process called permineralization. When a dinosaur dies, its bones may be buried by sediment, protecting them from decay. Over time, minerals from groundwater seep into the bones, replacing organic materials and turning them into rock-like fossils.

Preservation: The conditions during burial significantly affect the preservation of bones. Rapid burial in anoxic (low oxygen) environments enhances preservation, while exposure to air can lead to degradation.

Bone Structure Variability

Diversity: Different dinosaur species had distinct bone structures reflecting their size, lifestyle, and adaptations. For example, the thick, robust bones of heavy herbivores like *Triceratops* contrast sharply with the lighter, more elongated bones of agile theropods like *Velociraptor*.

Specialized Bones: Some dinosaurs had specialized bones for specific functions, such as the unique crests of *Parasaurolophus* and *Corythosaurus*, which likely played roles in communication or mating displays.

Pathologies and Injuries

Bone Pathologies: Fossilized dinosaur bones can show signs of disease or injury, providing insights into their health and behavior. For instance, some fossils exhibit evidence of bone infections, arthritis, or healed fractures, suggesting that dinosaurs experienced injuries and illnesses similar to modern animals.

Implications for Behavior: The presence of injuries may indicate behavioral traits, such as territorial battles or predatory attacks, offering clues about the social dynamics of various species.

Bone Histology

Microstructure Analysis: Scientists study the microstructure of dinosaur bones using techniques like histology to gain insights into their growth rates, metabolism, and physiology. This analysis helps determine whether a dinosaur was warm-blooded or cold-blooded based on the density and structure of its bones.

Bone Fossils in Context

Bonebeds: Sometimes, large numbers of dinosaur bones are found in one location, known as a bonebed. These deposits can indicate behaviors such as nesting, herd behavior, or mass mortality events, such as a catastrophic event leading to the death of many individuals at once.

Sedimentary Context: The geological context in which dinosaur bones are found can provide valuable information about the environment in which the dinosaurs lived. For example, bones found in river deposits may suggest a floodplain habitat.

Cultural Significance

Scientific Importance: Dinosaur bones are crucial for understanding the history of life on Earth and the evolution of species over millions of years. They form the basis of much of what we know about dinosaurs, their diversity, and their ecosystems.

Public Interest: Dinosaur bones capture the public's imagination, leading to numerous museums and educational programs aimed at sharing knowledge about these ancient creatures.

Dinosaur bones are not just remnants of the past; they are rich sources of information about the biology, behavior, and environment of dinosaurs. Through studying their composition, growth patterns, fossilization processes, and pathologies, scientists continue to uncover the mysteries of these ancient animals and their place in Earth's history.

Conclusion

Dinosaurs, the incredible rulers of the ancient world, continue to captivate our imaginations even millions of years after their extinction. Through the lens of scientific discovery, we have ventured into the diverse and fascinating realm of these creatures, exploring the vast array of species that once thrived on Earth. From towering giants to nimble predators, each type of dinosaur contributed to an intricate ecosystem that spanned millions of years.

The sudden extinction of these mighty creatures marked a turning point in Earth's history. The catastrophic asteroid impact, which created the Chicxulub crater, brought about swift and irreversible changes to the planet's environment. As we've seen, the aftermath of this event led to a mass extinction, where some dinosaurs perished early, while others held on until the very end. The extinction event remains one of the most significant mysteries of paleontology, but through careful research, we've gained valuable insights into who might have been the first and last to survive.

We've also explored the personalities of dinosaurs, from the most aggressive hunters to the calm herbivores that peacefully grazed the prehistoric landscapes.

Among the most intriguing are *Nigersaurus*, the dinosaur with 500 teeth, and the clawed *Therizinosaurus*, each offering unique adaptations that made them stand out in the dinosaur world.

In addition to their behavior, we've uncovered the secrets of how dinosaurs reproduced, examining their eggs, nests, and the possible parental care they provided to their young. These insights paint a picture of complex and intelligent creatures capable of nurturing their offspring.

While dinosaurs are often misunderstood in popular culture, this book has aimed to dispel many common misconceptions, revealing the true nature of these extraordinary animals. Dinosaur bones, meticulously studied over the years, continue to provide clues that enrich our understanding of their lives, growth, and extinction.

Although the age of dinosaurs has long passed, their legacy endures in the fossilized remains that tell their story. From their rise to their tragic fall, dinosaurs have left an indelible mark on the history of life on Earth. By studying their bones and uncovering their mysteries, we not only learn about the past but also gain a deeper appreciation for the forces that shape life on our planet.

As we close this journey through time, the story of dinosaurs reminds us that life on Earth is fragile, ever-changing, and full of wonder. While dinosaurs no longer walk the Earth, their impact remains with us, inspiring generations to explore, discover, and marvel at the natural world.

Milton Keynes UK
Ingram Content Group UK Ltd.
UKHW010923131024
449482UK00009B/41